Disclaimer

Your Gift

As a way of saying *thanks* for purchasing and reading this book, I am giving you a free gift and I invite you to take a look at my blog –
http://entrepreneurenhanced.com

*To get this gift click on the photo or click on the blog to sign up to my email list.

Contents

Chapter 1: Self-Publishing Tools
Chapter 2: Starting Your Blog
Chapter 3: What Makes a Blog Profitable
Chapter 4: Monetizing Your Blog
Chapter 5: Create Killer Content
Chapter 6: Pricing Strategies
Chapter 7: Tips
Chapter 8: Resources
Other Books By Ryan Stevens
Last Word

Chapter 1: Self-Publishing Tools

Once upon time, traditional publishers had to spend a lot of time writing their books, doing research, editing drafts (without having the modern tools we have today), and of course, they weren't able to make too much money.

Yes, it's sad and unfair for popular writers like Jules Verne or William Shakespeare to barely make a living out of their writing. Like most of the writers, they've become popular and their work has been appreciated just after they passed away. Totally unfair, they were simply brilliant.

I just named two popular writers, there are thousands of traditional writers who continue even today to write the same as before and even if they're brilliant, they aren't capable of making a lot of money.

Why do you think they didn't make enough money?

- *They weren't able to share their work globally at the same time (like we can do today because of Internet expansion)*
- *Writing a book back then takes a lot more time than it does today.*
- *They had to edit/proofread their work by themselves.*
- *They had to run through several approvals until they're work became available for purchase.*
- *Limited sources of inspiration*
- *No global approach (no Internet)*

There are dozens of reasons why it was a lot harder than today. Right now, people are consuming information on a daily basis, even without realizing it - social media, eBooks, posts, websites, books, e-courses, videos, etc.

Self-publishing is not the only profitable market today, a lot of businesses that focus on the Internet are profitable and generally have a big potential of success. Most of the online businesses are successful because they're using a few tools which, in my opinion, are crucial. Tools like:

- *a blog/website*
- *an email list*
- *lead magnets*
- *search engines*
- *social media*
- *adverts*
- *outsourcing services*
- *online platforms*

In this small booklet, I will mainly discuss blogging and how to use/build your blog if you are a self-publisher (and not only). I will cover how to start a blog in the next chapter.

Chapter 2: Starting Your Blog

Starting a blog or a website is really easy, most of the times it can be done all at once within an hour or two. I will cover all the expenses, all the websites where you need to go and other helpful resources.

Here's exactly what you need:

- *Domain*
- *Hosting*
- *Theme*
- *WordPress installation*
- *Setting everything up*

The domain is the name of your website, so what you need to do first is to find out a great name which fits your niche/topic. If you write about science-fiction, try to find the best match and also look for keywords related to science fiction (using Google Keyword Planner - it's free). Let's say the name sci-fi-addicted.com is available and you decide to purchase it. Domains are cheap, sometimes ridiculously cheap - they're usually around $12/year, but if you find a great deal at GoDaddy for example, you can pick one for $2.99/year (the first year). Let's assume it costs $12.

Now that you have a domain, you need someone to host your website 24/7, so we need to purchase web hosting or WordPress hosting. We have multiple options:

- *Bluehost*
- *Hostgator*
- *GoDaddy*
- *Other*

My personal option is GoDaddy - it's fast, it's cheap, didn't have any issues with them at all, etc. Basic hosting with GoDaddy is only $3.99/month and you have 10GB of SSD storage (really quick, pages load faster) and up to 25,000 visitors a month. From my experience and from what I studied on the web, it takes a lot of effort to beat those numbers, I would say you need at least 2 years of daily work to exceed 25,000 a month, and if you do, all I have to say is *Congratulations, you have a successful blog!*

Now let's continue with the math, for $3.99/month, you need $47.88/year, but I always purchase every 3 months ($15.96/3 months). This totals $59.88/year or $4.99/month. Now let's face it, everybody can afford this small fee to run a blog with your own custom domain.

Soon after you purchase all of these, you need to login into your GoDaddy account and then install WordPress. Now, go to your dashboard (http://sci-fi-addicted.com/wp-admin) and play with the menu - you can create pages, posts, links, add media, customize everything, add widgets, plugins, etc.

Your blog/website is currently empty and has no theme. If you have the money, I would recommend buying a custom theme from http://themeforest.com, which are from $20 to $100 (in average). I paid a theme which cost me $57 including VAT, but I must admit that I am not totally happy with it.

Customize the appearance, buttons, colors, widgets and add a few plugins such as:

Next, I will discuss what makes a blog profitable and successful.

Chapter 3: What Makes a Blog Profitable

It's quite difficult these days to start a blog without having any idea what you're doing. It takes a lot of time and patience until you start making money and it can take years until you can make a full living just from blogging.

But here's the magic - having a blog for a self-publisher can be truly powerful and I will explain why. When you have just a blog, you're mainly focusing on organic traffic from Google and even if it's OK, it takes too much time until you reach a decent number of daily visitors.

As a self-publisher (fiction or nonfiction author), you can write a series of books on a topic/niche and offer 1-2 books or even more for free on multiple platforms -

Kindle, Smashwords, etc. The traffic from those books can be easily sent to your blog and you can make a lot of traffic (20-30% of the people who download the book for free will check out your website).

It depends on the topic you choose, but generally, you will make around 50 - 100 free units just on Amazon so 15 to 30 people will go to your blog daily and 50% of those will sign up to your newsletter/email list. Remember that these numbers are just from 1 free book. What if you create 5 in a row on similar topics. Those books take around 3 months to write and self-publish and they could easily generate 200 free units/day and 100 visitors/day to your blog. That's 3000/month which is great for the beginning.

If you reserve 2 hours a day for your blog - 1 hour to write your blog posts and 1 hour for writing guest posts, comments on different related to your topic, you can make another 50-100 visitors/day within 3 months just from Google's search engines.

Joining forums related to your niche is another great way to boost your traffic - 90% of your comments will stay there permanently, so whenever someone searches for something on that forum, your post will appear.

Social media, YouTube videos, and Udemy are another great sources of free traffic. It takes time until you publish videos, create accounts and finishing a course, but on the long-term, your traffic will skyrocket.

Paying for advertising is another great way to make traffic. The most effective way to do this is by using Facebook ads. Now, if you're a self-publisher, don't send the traffic to your books which require money to purchase, try sending them to something free - your blog, your lead magnet or a free book on Amazon.

Now, let's sum up.

As a self-publisher you have the advantage of using all these at once - write a few free books for traffic, sign up to multiple social media platforms, write blog posts (2-3/week), write guest posts or comments every day (at least 1-2/day), create a YouTube video (1/week) and after a while create a free Udemy course (after 3-4 months) and share your experience.

The only way in which you will be successful with all these techniques is when you will help others. Even if your work is free, make sure to deliver high-quality content and a "premium" experience to your readers or customers.

Take as an example this free book - it's short but I believe it's valuable for starters, I have a blog, I have an email list and I constantly upload blog posts, articles, books (free & paid) and I put a lot of effort in everything I do.

I believe that if you follow this piece of advice, you will be averaging +300 visitors/month within 3 months which is blazing fast. Believe it or not, I am doing the same thing. Obviously, by having visitors from your books and from your posts, people will be interested in signing up to your email list for offers, bargains, free content and tips. Having 300 visitors a day or even more will result in at least 30-40 subscribers per day and if you use paid advertising, number can easily grow.

Facebook advertising allows you to target specific audiences (which may interest you) and from what I know, with $1,000 you can generate around 3,000 to 5,000 subscribers. It may sound a lot, but those subscribers will make you a lot of money on the long run. *You know what they say, the money is in the list.*

What's also important is to mention your blog and free offer (lead magnet) in all your books, whether they are paid or free. Being able to sell 200-300 copies a month from all your titles will also result in at least 10% conversion to your email list.

In the next chapter, I will discuss different ways of monetizing your blog.

Chapter 4: Monetizing Your Blog

A blog is meant to offer free content, offer advice, experience and any kind of free (and useful) information but we simply can't do everything forever for free, right?

First of all, a professional blog or a professional website which gets traffic and hosts your stuff requires money to run. SEO optimization, domain, hosting, professional email (for email marketing), email marketing services, proofreading content (optional), advertising, graphics (design, theme), and more, require in average nearly $100/month.

So how can we monetize our work?

I want to mention that there are hundreds of ways of monetizing your blog, but there are a few which are the most popular and some of them are really profitable.

Here are a few ways of monetizing a blog:

1. *Google AdSense* - this is one of the most common ways, but I honestly don't recommend it. You get a ridiculously low bid (especially at the beginning) and you need at least 1,000 visitors a day just to cover your monthly expenses (of around $100 per month). Also, Google Ads are so annoying when a visitor comes to your blog and gets suffocated by all kinds of adverts.

2. *Affiliate marketing* - this can include an insanely big list of places/products/services/websites you can promote on your blog. The most profitable and the best affiliate marketing platform is Amazon through its Associates program. You basically get between 4 and 8% depending on what you advertise and how many products you sell a month. Depending on the topic of your blog, you can find different partners to promote or different similar websites for which you can become an affiliate.

Let's take an example - I self-publish books, I can become an affiliate for CreateSpace (for every person who signs up through your affiliate link, you get $8) , iWriter (you get 50% of the earnings of the iWriter team - if someone writes an article of $10 and iWriter gets $2, you get $1), Archangel Ink (editing company), BuckBooks (you need to give them subscribers and get $1 for each), Kindle (promoting a Kindle device can give you serious commissions + promoting your own books through Associates gives you another 4% royalty), Evernote (you don't get money, but you get free premium months of usage), etc. It all depends on your blog's topic - you are responsible for choosing your own affiliate partners, but the point is that you can make money on any topic through affiliate marketing).

3. Email marketing - this is mainly based on affiliate marketing, but you can seriously boost everything up. Some people have huge email lists (+100,000 subscribers) and just by sending an email with a few links and a product review will generate at least 1% sales. This equates to at least 1,000 potential customers who purchase in the following hour something. If you get in average a $5 commission, just from 1 email you can earn $5,000, think how powerful this is!

4. Promote your own products - most of the professional bloggers have eBooks, their own products, courses, coaching services, etc. and the traffic from the blog promotes their offer.

I would say that most important and profitable way to make money from a blog is from affiliate marketing. It's vast, profitable and the key to making a blog profitable.

I would highly recommend you not to use Google AdSense - you're making visitors leave your blog (you increase the bounce rate) rather than having a great, clean experience and transforming them into potential subscribers/customers.

Chapter 5: Create Killer Content

Quality is a major player in any business. If you want to succeed and to constantly drive organic traffic to your website/blog, you need to come up with original, high-quality content.

What this means is that you need to publish 1-3 posts every week and each post should have between 750 and 1500 words (what's less than 750 is a joke and what's more than 1500 gets boring at some point for a single blog post).

However, it's not just about the number of blog posts or about the length, you need to deliver value, you need to help others with your posts. If you're not doing this, people will leave, people will write negative reviews or comments and your traffic (business) will go down. It's only a matter of time.

Here are 5 tips to implement while you write a new blog post:

1. Note down every idea that you have using a note taking app (such as Evernote).

This happens to me all the time. When I want to write something down, I don't have all the necessary information in mind at once, so I always tend to note down on my phone whenever I have a new suggestion for my blog post or for anything related to my business. Now, don't think that I am writing the whole blog post in the note, I'm just writing some keywords, some titles and probably some resources (or links).

2. Include affiliate links to products you used in the past (don't include too many, it's annoying).

As I said in the previous chapters, the most important and the most profitable stream for a blog is affiliate marketing. Make sure you include a few links to your own products (slightly introduce them before introducing any links) and don't exaggerate with them.

3. Use a friendly tone.

Use a "warm voice" in your posts and from time to time use humor. Most of the successful people do this (including Bill Gates).

4. Make sure your posts are error free.

Ughh. Errors. I don't claim that my blog/books/services are perfect. There's no such thing as perfection, but too many errors will make your readers go away, so just be careful and make sure to check your content before uploading.

5. Write guest posts and invite others to write guest posts to your blog for more traffic.

Chapter 6: Pricing Strategies

Pricing can be quite tricky when it comes to getting new customers. The truth is that we need to create an offer which starts from the bottom (free) to the top (high-end offer) in order to obtain the best profits and reach the highest number of customers/readers.

This can be used for any kind of business, but it's crucial for a blogger or for a person who publishes books on Kindle. Let's take it from the start.

When you create a blog, you are basically offering content (thoughts, case studies, experiences, articles, news, etc.) for free. We do this to get traffic, to try to solve someone's problem and to hope that they will be coming back (again, for traffic).

The next question - what do we do with traffic? We are trying to convert the traffic into potential subscribers or followers, and eventually, we are trying to convert subscribers into customers for profit.

As a blogger and self-publisher (like me), you are trying to focus on 3 things - traffic, income and subscribers. To do this, we need to price everything differently - from $0.00 to $9.99 (or more).

Let's say you have 2 free books, 2 books at $0.99, 5 at $2.99, one at $4.99 and one at $9.99. People who don't trust you or don't know anything about you will initially get the free books and the $0.99 books. If they will like your content and if you help them out with something, they will want more and they might consider the $2.99 books. If they're even more satisfied with the content and the value that you provide, then you've won their trust and they will purchase all your books and maybe every book that you release. These people will be your loyal subscribers who will constantly follow and support you.

It's very hard (sometimes quite impossible) to win someone's trust by offering him a $100 product.

In our days, the best way to attract someone is by offering something for free - a course, a video or a book.

In other words, whatever you do (sell courses, sell books, create a blog), make sure to include these:

- *Free offer*
- *Entry level offer*
- *Mid-range offer (or core offer)*
- *High-end offer*

This system is just like a pyramid - the base is Free and the top is the high-end. If you're not following this plan and you're trying to make money from selling 2-3 high-end products without having any kind of audience or authority, then you're wasting your time.

On the other hand, if you're just offering free stuff or entry level stuff ($0.99 books), it will be nearly impossible to become financially free (cover all your expenses) from what you're doing. The best way to attract people, make money, gain trust and build a solid business is to create a variety of different products priced differently which target similar categories of people.

Chapter 7: Tips

1. Write in the morning

You're full of energy and full of ideas in the morning, so use them wisely by creating new content. Whether you're writing a blog post, you send an email or you're writing a book, it seems that most of the authors and entrepreneurs are more productive if they write soon after they wake up.

2. Invite others to write guest posts

While you help others boost their blogs, you will also take advantage of the traffic which come from others' posts. Create a dedicated button in your menu called "Guest Posts" and let others share their work.

3. Promote only products you love or have knowledge about

If you're willing to create an affiliate marketing business by using your blog or you simply want to increase your income, make sure to promote things you like. For example, I am very interested in tech (accessories, laptops, smartphones, gadgets), watches or car accessories (windshield holder for tablets, snow chains, etc.).

4. Promote products which cost $50 or more

While Affiliate Marketing is profitable these days, I suppose you wouldn't like to promote a product that costs $1.50 knowing that Amazon generally gives you a 4% commission. How would it convert, 6 cents commission? I'm not saying to promote products which cost thousands of dollars, but $50-$300 is the best range for Amazon Associates.

5. *Promote your own books with Amazon Associates*

While you earn another 4% on each sale, users can also buy additional items from which you get a commission. For instance, if you promote your book which is about "Weight Loss", some folks would probably consider purchasing a *Digital Weight Bathroom Scale* or someone else's book or some weight loss pills or some trainers, a tracksuit, etc.

For each individual item purchased within 24 hours from your affiliate link, you get a commission. It doesn't matter if someone goes to Amazon trough your link and buys something else, you still get a commission.

If customers go to Amazon through your affiliate link and add products (within 24 hours) to cart and they buy that products within 30 days, you still get a commission.

6. Don't include affiliate links in your emails

If you built an email list, don't send affiliate links to them - firstly, if Amazon finds out about it, you will get banned from the program and secondly, your subscribers will be more likely to unsubscribe.

7. Don't include affiliate links in you kindle books or any ebooks.

It's against Amazon's TOS to include affiliate links in Kindle books. You can include back links from your books to your blog and from your blog to Amazon products through the Associates program.

8. Promote everything related to your niche

Create new partners, sign up to affiliate offers and always experiment. While you create new relationships with other platforms, they might promote your brand or blog too.

9. Constantly improve yourself and your business

There's no such thing as perfection and we don't need to be perfect to start a new business, but you might want to take into consideration investing a few pennies in yourself and in your blog - new books, seminars, webinars, courses, blog design, etc.

Chapter 8: Resources

In this last chapter, I will include resources and links to what you need for your blog.

Hosting & Domain

- GoDaddy   -
  https://www.godaddy.com/
- Bluehost   -
  https://www.bluehost.com/
- HostGator   -
  http://www.hostgator.com/

Note - After purchasing the domain and hosting, login in your host's account, download and install WordPress.

Email Marketing Services

- AWeber - https://www.aweber.com
- MailChimp - http://mailchimp.com/
- Benchmark Email - http://www.benchmarkemail.com/

Self-Publishing Platforms

- Amazon Kindle Publishing - https://kdp.amazon.com/
- SmashWords - https://www.smashwords.com/
- Apple - http://www.apple.com/ibooks-author/
- Nook - http://www.barnesandnoble.com/

On Demand Publishing (Print)

- CreateSpace - https://www.createspace.com/

- LuLu - https://www.lulu.com/

Courses (Free & Paid)

- Udemy - https://www.udemy.com/courses/

Advertising

- Fiverr (Paid ads or services)
- YouTube (Free Channel)
- Twitter (Ads)
- LinkedIn (Ads)
- Udemy (Free Course)
- Facebook (Ads)
- Amazon Marketing Services (AMS Ads)
- Amazon Author Central (visibility)
- Goodreads (Ads)
- Google+

Forums (suitable for Forum Marketing)

- Warrior Forum - https://www.warriorforum.com/

- Kindle Boards - http://kboards.com/

Affiliate Marketing

- Amazon Associates Program - https://affiliate-program.amazon.com/
- Clickbank - http://www.clickbank.com/
- CreateSpace - https://www.createspace.com/
- Udemy - https://www.udemy.com/courses/
- BuckBooks - http://buckbooks.net/
- GoDaddy - https://www.godaddy.com/
- Bluehost - https://www.bluehost.com/

Book Formatting & Editing

- Upwork - https://www.upwork.com/
- Freelancer - https://www.freelancer.com
- Fiverr - https://www.fiverr.com/
- Archangel Ink - http://archangelink.com/

Cover Design

- Fiverr - https://www.fiverr.com/
- Upwork - https://www.upwork.com/
- 99designs - http://99designs.com/
- CreateSpace Team - https://www.createspace.com/
- Archangel Ink - http://archangelink.com/

Reviews (Real honest reviews)

- Reading Deals - http://readingdeals.com/
- Goodreads - http://www.goodreads.com/

Book Promotion Websites

- eBooksHabit - http://ebookshabit.com/
- Reading Deals - http://readingdeals.com/
- Fiverr - https://www.fiverr.com/
- Buck Books - http://buckbooks.net/
- Books Butterfly - http://www.booksbutterfly.com/order/
- Kindle Boards (Ads) - http://www.kboards.com/ads/
- Facebook (Ads) - https://www.facebook.com/ads/manager

- Digital Book Today - http://digitalbooktoday.com/
- Book Marketing Tools - http://bookmarketingtools.com/
- BargainBooksy - http://www.bargainbooksy.com/
- FreeBooksy - http://www.freebooksy.com/
- ENT - E-Reader News Today - http://ereadernewstoday.com/
- BookBub - https://www.bookbub.com/partners/pricing
- Many Books - http://manybooks.net/
- Genre Pulse - http://www.genrepulse.com/
- Bargain Book Hunter - http://bargainebookhunter.com/
- Pixel Scroll - http://pixelscroll.com/

- Bookgoodies - http://bookgoodies.com/
- eReaderGirl - http://ereadergirl.com/
- Read Cheaply - http://readcheaply.com/
- eBookHounds - http://www.ebookhounds.com/
- eBookSoda - http://www.ebooksoda.com/
- eBook Lister - http://www.ebooklister.net/
- BookSends - http://booksends.com/
- Daily Cheap Reads - http://www.dailycheapreads.com/
- Fussy Librarian - http://www.thefussylibrarian.com/
- One Hundred Free Books - http://ohfb.com/

- Free eBooks Daily - http://www.freeebooksdaily.com/

Site Ranking

- Alexa - http://www.alexa.com/

Other Books By Ryan Stevens

[FREE eBook] - 33 Self-Publishing Tips

A short read with 33 tips for a brand new self-publisher.

[50% OFF - Box Set] - Premium Self-Publishing Bundle

- CreateSpace Publishing For Independent Self-Publishers
- Entrepreneur Enhanced
- Kindle Publishing PRO
- Online Startup
- Express Book Launch

Amazon Associates Affiliate Program

Learn what Affiliate Marketing is, how it is done and how you can start your own.

[$0.99 Book] - Online Startup – How To Make Money Online Even When You Don't Have Any

Most startups require money, so to initially make money, start from the bottom. Use the information within this book and use the simplest method to make money online even today.

[$0.99 Book] - CreateSpace For Independent Self-Publishers

Nowadays, people prefer to buy digital eBooks instead of physical ones because it's faster, cheaper, environmentally friendly, and you theoretically have unlimited stock. However, there still are people who prefer physical books and they pay for them even though they're more   expensive.
You can publish just on CreateSpace or you can publish on both Kindle and CreateSpace (I recommend doing both).

Evernote In 90 Minutes Or Less

Not only can you find unlimited ways of using this app for de-cluttering and organizing your life, but while you do that, developers will also find more ways to improve it and add more features to it.

Express Book Launch

Launching a book on Amazon is a complex strategy that takes months to be correctly understood. For most authors on Amazon, this has been the most challenging process of the business.

Entrepreneur Enhanced

You don't have to be an expert, and you don't have to be perfect in what you do; you only need to be committed to what you do. You have to always push and move on, no matter what happens. Nobody said that it will be easy to become an entrepreneur. "Now" is the right time to get started.

Kindle Publishing PRO

Unlike other books that regurgitate the same information because they're written by inexperienced publishers, this guide will give you the key information from an author who has done it time and time again. Just a few years ago, the idea of publishing a book was far out of reach for most everyone, but with the help of this giant online marketplace, you can quickly and safely publish your own book and make a profit!

More will come up soon, sign up to my newsletter for offers at $0.99 or FREE books – *http://entrepreneurenhanced.com*

Last Word

The modern writer/author/self-publisher has to be an entrepreneur, too. If you focus just on writing, who will take care of the other tasks?

I've seen authors who have pure talent for writing, but they can't get in touch with someone to promote them. However, I've also seen self-publishers who weren't that great, but they had a huge audience behind them and they made a lot of money by taking advantage of it.

The modern self-publisher needs to be an "authorpreneur" to succeed and to make over 4 figures a month from self-publishing.

The top 3 tools for a self-publisher (as I mentioned earlier) are a *blog*, an *email* list, and *social media*. You simply can't succeed without them.

I tried as much as possible to make this booklet compact and straight to the point, so I hope you learned something from it.

You can follow me and subscribe to my newsletter (check the free gift at the beginning of this book) and you'll receive valuable information, free or discounted books at $0.99.

If you think that this book has been useful to you, I kindly ask you to write a short review. By doing this, you will help me improve myself and my books and you will also help me reach more readers just like you.

Regards,
Ryan